an extract
jonathan falla's

blue poppies

with an enthusiast's view
by rosemary goring

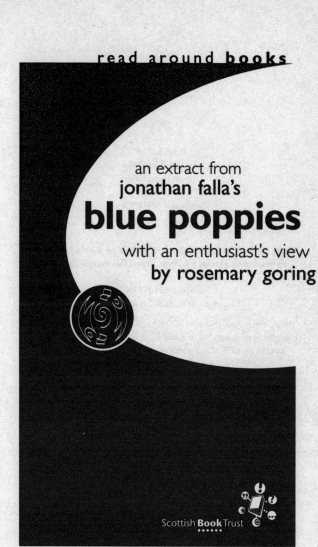

an extract from
jonathan falla's
blue poppies
with an enthusiast's view
by rosemary goring

Scottish **Book** Trust

2003

Published by
Scottish Book Trust
Scottish Book Centre
137 Dundee Street
Edinburgh EH11 1BG

Tel: 0131 229 3663

**From April 2003 Scottish Book Trust will be moving its offices
to Sandeman House, 55 High Street, Edinburgh EH1 1SR.**

ISBN: 1 901077 04 7
Copyright © Scottish Book Trust, 2003

Published with the support of the Scottish Arts Council National
Lottery Fund and The Hugh Fraser Foundation.

Blue Poppies is published by 11:9, an imprint of NWP Ltd
ISBN: 1 903238 5 52

Extract copyright © Jonathan Falla, 2001

Series design by Caleb Rutherford   eidetic
Printed in the UK by Cox & Wyman, Reading, Berkshire

contents

read **around books**

There is no shortage of fiction on the shelves of our bookshops – quite the opposite – but finding one that shouts out 'this is what you are looking for' is getting harder and harder as the number of books published goes up with each passing year. Too often we open a new book with expectation and enthusiasm only to discover disappointment and to struggle to get beyond page thirty. When we do find a book we really enjoy the urge is there to tell friends, colleagues and family to read it too in the hope that they will share our delight.

Read Around Books goes one step further and puts that enthusiasm down in black and white in the hope that many more readers will discover the joys of reading the very finest fiction that has emerged from Scotland over the last one hundred years. **This is a chance to sample before you borrow or buy**. Others have found these books before you, the writing held them spellbound and even when finished, these books would not let their readers go.

Each of the first twelve of these highly collectable little guide books promotes a work of fiction by a writer who lives in Scotland, was born in Scotland or who has been influenced by Scotland (our definition of Scottish is generous). Together they offer a marvellous introduction to the very best of Scottish writing from the twentieth and the first few years of the twenty-first centuries.

In each you will find a substantial extract, the enthusiast's view of the book, starting points for discussion for readers' groups, a short biographical piece about the author, and suggestions for similar reads which act as a further gateway to fine fiction.

Jan Rutherford
Series editor, 2003

the enthusiast

Rosemary Goring

Rosemary Goring is Literary Editor of *The Herald* newspaper.

the enthusiast's **view**

Blue Poppies
by Jonathan Falla

A powerful story of war and love, *Blue Poppies* has few of the hallmarks of the debut novel. It is neither autobiographical nor therapeutic, pyrotechnic nor experimental. Instead it is a work of calm passion, clearly inspired by the author's love for the landscape and people of Tibet. As the story unfolds, peopled with complex, strong-minded personalities, none is more striking or plays a larger role than that of the country, whose harsh and beautiful terrain is mirrored in the behaviour and beliefs of the protagonists.

There could hardly be a more striking backdrop for fiction. Set in the years 1948 to 1950, *Blue Poppies* is the story of the remote Tibetan village of Jyeko, tucked away in the eastern province of Kham, close to the Chinese border. It is a land of medieval poverty and superstition. Tibetan buddhism is the religion, its flame kept burning by hard-working lamas who live closely alongside their people, leaving their lamasary each day to mingle with the villagers, yet unable to rid them of their ignorant fears, no matter how much they preach the message of peace and tolerance, no matter how many prayer flags they encourage the villagers to display or sticks of incense they ask them to burn.

Falla's knowledge of the area is luminous, lifting his tale from the ordinary into a realm of its own. Seemingly casual references to mountain weather, distinctive wildlife, such as the pica – a tiny creature part mouse part rabbit – and rare flowers, such as the medicinal blue poppies of the title, colour the narrative like a mountain sky over water, shaping the prose and the plot.

The Tibetan landscape offers visions of otherworldly loveliness matched by life-threatening danger. *Blue Poppies*, not surprisingly, is a tale of conflict, between love and fear, desire and anger. Every sentence is underpinned by tension, the personal battles of its main characters set against the wider picture of a threatened nation striving to maintain its independence.

The first hint that life will soon change in the ancient backwater of Jyeko is the arrival of a recently demobbed Scottish wireless operator. Jamie Wilson, an energetic 22-year-old from Inverkeithing, is known to the locals as the Ying-gi-li. A former member of the Royal Corps of Signals who has served in Palestine and Malaya, Jamie is on a civilian contract to provide radio service to the region. The remoteness of Jyeko does not bother him. In fact, the wilder the place, the better he loves it. 'His spirit was free and his curiosity without limit.'

After the claustrophobic comforts of home in 'a suburb of tight-lipped Episcopalian tradesmen' Jamie is bitten with wanderlust. For him, Jyeko is one more notch on his ambitious itinerary. While he may enjoy its eccentricities and revel in his easy friendships, he recognises that he will always only be a stranger, at best a welcome guest. For a long time he is glad to be detached, not responsible for anyone but himself. It is only one of the many small emotional detonations in the novel when he begins to realise that 'the more he moved on, the lonelier he'd be'.

As well as his radio, Jamie brings with him a breath of the 20th century to a people cut off for generations from technological advance. When the monks hear of his arrival they ask, 'What is radio?'. When the procedure is explained, they remain uneasy. 'Are the spirits of the upper air disturbed?'

Such ignorance might seem charming, but very soon Jamie feels the chill of more primitive ways. In the village, some time earlier, a tax inspector had arrived, with his wife and child. Bitterly resented by the villagers, the inspector met with a fatal accident when riding along a gorge path. During the incident, his wife was badly hurt. By the time Jamie arrives, this unfortunate widow's crushed leg has been healed by one of the lamas, Khempo Nima, who from that time watches out for her safety.

A handsome woman, called Puton, she is seen as an omen of ill-fortune and shunned by her neighbours and landlord who believe she'll bring bad luck. Hirpling around on a crutch, trying to scrape a living for herself and her very young daughter, Puton is close to despair when Khempo Nima takes her to live with Jamie as his housekeeper. 'They will be family for you', he says, meaningfully, as he settles the pair in Jamie's backroom without any discussion.

It is one of the many attractive qualities of this novel that Falla does not strive for dramatic effect. The growing rapport between the reluctant Jamie, who doesn't think he needs a housekeeper, and the nervous Puton, who fears being kicked out, is delicately handled, understated and hesitant, as suits a couple who on first glance have nothing in common except a gentle disposition and a shared roof.

Puton is an enigmatic, proud but lovable character, a stoic who recognises that throughout her life she has never been the one to make a decision about her fate but has always been forced to rely on the actions of men. Such enforced subordination left her with only one avenue of response: 'She asked only the liberty to look on the inevitable with whatever face she chose.'

We are not given much overt insight into her thoughts, but the most descriptive glimpse we have offers a view of a woman of great loyalty and great sensual need. The developing bond between her and Jamie leaves her 'in the grip of a pretty imp that swarmed on her breast, frightening and delighting her all at once. But when this happy imp approached her heart, three dragons with spiny green tails, bloodshot eyes and toxic breath barred the door.

'The first was Malice, which would do her good name to death. The second was Desertion, the day she might find her protectors gone. The third was Reproach, which stirred each night: in a vision of a gorge, a storm of black rocks, a horse and a man falling with his cry lost in the roar of water.

'She would wake under the sheepskins, sweating, suffocating. She would light a lamp for comfort and lie motionless, listening to Dechen's easy breathing. And she would wonder how she could tell her husband that she honoured him still, to give him rest.'

Her dependent position is pitiably vulnerable, soon to be echoed by the plight of the whole of Tibet. Several months into the story, in January 1950, the Chinese Liberation Army is given its New Year task: 'the liberation of Taiwan and Tibet'. Not long after, Communists march into the village, and the lives of every villager, not just Jamie and Puton, are changed forever.

The compelling characterisation of the lamas, the villagers, and the hero and heroine are the product of Falla's clear-eyed compassion and fair-mindedness. When the Chinese enter Jyeko, they are not stock figures from a military school of caricature. The Captain who sets in train the disastrous events of the next few weeks is an honourable man, within his understanding of morality, more upstanding and civilised than many of the peasants in the village, despite the dictates of his military role.

As the events of war overtake Jamie and Puton, Falla focuses on Jamie's confusion, his contradictory feelings towards the backward people of Jyeko whom he by turns admires and despises. His loathing of them is also turned on himself. The only figure who emerges unscathed from his introspection is Puton, whose unwavering love and self-abnegation transform the selfish young man into a mature adult who begins to understand that he cannot go through life without making powerful attachments, whether to place or people.

There is an old-fashioned mood to this tale, partly perhaps a product of its setting, in an undeveloped country fifty years ago. But there is more purpose behind the classic tone than this alone. The elements of *Blue Poppies* are timeless: immovable mountains, age-long beliefs, and the implacable forces of prejudice which have not changed down the centuries. Though the lovingly described domestic details and crisp conversations between characters clearly reveal the age they depict, the structure and arc of the story could be that of ancient myth: an unconventional love affair; a village threatened by the advance of modern life; a country at the mercy of a well-marshalled enemy with superior forces.

It is no small feat for an author to combine seamlessly period fact and environmental detail with a profoundly moving, intimate personal drama. In Falla's hands, the majestic, awe-inspiring landscape of the Tibetan mountains in no way diminishes the puny affairs of the humans in its shadow. Rather, it enhances their relationships. By offering a backdrop that is immutable and untameable, Falla raises the stakes, both emotional and spiritual, of the love between Jamie and Puton, between the villagers and their country. The result is high octane fiction for a high altitude land.

The extract

Blue Poppies

Part three

one

They rode hard, not daring to glance behind them. A score of Khampa families with a dozen monks and a Scottish radio operator drove their animals forward in a clamour of shouts and whistles. The noise was unnecessary, since the animals moved readily enough, but it was preferable to the clamour of regret. In the centre of the crowd rode Jamie. On Khenpo Nima's instructions, two novices kept near to him. He did not appear to notice them, or anyone or anything else.

A short distance from the village, the trail began its diagonal climb up the mountain flank towards the first pass. The throng turned to single file on the narrow track. At the crest of the pass, two miles from the village and several hundred feet higher, the broad saddle was covered with a dusting of snow through which dead yellow grasses stuck. Here, the lead riders paused.

At last, they looked back. Almost everyone they knew was strung along the trail and climbing towards them. As each family reached the summit they, too, turned to gaze at the distant village, every detail visible in this thin, clean air. Nothing seemed out of the ordinary, except for the unusual quantity of prayer flags that still hung on every house, across every gate to keep the Chinese out. But scarcely a living soul was visible in the lanes. No children played, there were no dogs, no traders or market wives, no animals, no smoke from fires.

As Jamie and the villagers gathered in silence and looked down, a delicate sound reached them in faint wisps and snatches. It was a tiny ringing pain, trembling with unhappiness. A light wind was rising along the river valley, passing through the village towards the pass. As it went among the deserted houses, it had found a hundred little prayer bells on cords and springs in courtyards, windows and doorways. Touched and shaken, the shivering of these bells reached the people in the pass.

Khenpo Nima bit his lip and looked around the crowd. He saw a strong man raise a hand slowly to his face. A girl wept noiselessly and twisted a cloth tighter and tighter in whitened fists. Then a woman began to move, leading a mule with two children. She had turned round, back down the mountainside towards her home. A moment later, her husband started after her, hauling a yak on which all their possessions teetered. No one spoke, but Nima felt that everyone held their breath. In a minute, the family was a hundred yards below them, racing for Jyeko on lurching animals.

Khenpo Nima swung down off his pony and picked up a large flatstone in his broad hands. There was a high cairn at the crest of the pass. Nima strode towards it purposefully, pulling his mount after him. He slapped the stone onto the cairn with all the decisiveness and noise he could manage, shouting: 'The gods are victorious, the devils are defeated!'

They'd all cried it a thousand times, a tradition for the crossing of a pass. No one moved. Khenpo Nima surveyed them in dismay. Then Karjen stooped also and picked up a fat little boulder. He hoisted his rock to the cairn's top and bellowed the same: 'The gods are victorious, the devils are defeated!'

At last, the villagers began to stir. Everyone, every family found a rock for the cairn; even small children seated on yaks were given little stones and shown where to toss them. The cry was repeated, and repeated. So the village began to pick their way down the far side of the pass.

*

They travelled fifteen miles in the first day. The ground was hard and level; the caravan spread out, allowing the animals to nose for fodder. At dusk, they set up camp. Some of the shelters were huge, stout felt raised on ropes over outer poles, with all the appearance of black spiders in the snow. These were tents for wintering out, gale-proof and clan capacity. But many of the townspeople had only light summer pavilions, or the little ridge tents of brown hemp cloth the herdsmen carried to pasture, open to the wind at one end.

With fires lit and tea prepared, the villagers had time at last to talk, to reassure each other that they'd acted wisely. Khenpo Nima saw Jamie by a family cooking fire. Karjen was busily repairing a rip in the tent they'd borrowed so these people had given Jamie food. He sat in silence. The daylight failed, the herdsmen drove their animals together and volunteers stood watch. There were leopards in the hills they'd passed through. Brown bears, quick to kill mules, ponies, sheep, had been seen in the distance that afternoon. In the borrowed tent, Jamie, Karjen and a herdsman lay packed between bags of food and the boxed radio equipment. Around them, the children's cries died down, until the only sounds were the stamps and shufflings of ponies, gruff snorts from the yaks and soft speech at the watch fires.

So a routine began. It would take many weeks to draw near to Lhasa, even if the winter weather was kind.

They rose and ate at dawn, then began the elaborate business of repacking. The herdsmen were ready to move well before the villagers, and drove their ponderous yaks on to the trail while some families were still eating. Once re-formed, the caravan stayed together: the old perils of the road – bandits, wolves – were still there. Now many of the travellers were quiet, deep in their thoughts. Again they camped; again they moved on.

Mid-morning on the third day, there came a shout from the lead riders. A few hundred yards ahead, a small party of two or three families had appeared, leading pack animals on foot. At the sight of the Jyeko caravan, these people began to run. They turned off the main track to head across the empty plain.

'Perhaps they think we're Chinese,' said Khenpo Nima doubtfully.

Wangdu shouted: 'Akung, Norbu! Go after them!'

Several young men spurred away in pursuit; Khenpo Nima saw the Jyeko horsemen cut in front of the strangers, wheel about and lean down from their saddles to talk. While he watched, he noticed Jamie bring his pony nearer, ready to listen. Then the riders returned.

'What's happening? Do they take us for bandits or what?' called Karjen.

The young men's faces were flushed. 'There's news,' they began.

'Doubtless,' retorted Wangdu. 'Where are they from?'

'Near Chamdo. There's been a battle! Thousands of Chinese, they're everywhere! They've taken Chamdo!'

'Taken it?' growled Karjen. 'Somebody gave it to them?'

The information tumbled out in a tangle. 'They weren't prepared, everyone has left, they blew up the magazines!'

'For pity's sake,' interrupted Khenpo Nima, 'one thing at a time.'

The boys glanced at each other, then began again: 'Five days ago, Governor Ngabo heard that the Chinese had crossed the river at Batang, so he fled. The Khampas wanted to fight, they wanted the ammunition in the magazine. But the Governor wouldn't give it, and he fled. Then the Chinese attacked Chamdo at night, and now it's all over, finished.'

'What's finished?'

'They caught Governor Ngabo. The Chinese have got him. We've surrendered.'

'Speak for yourself,' said Karjen. 'That's what happens when you have a ponce from Lhasa in charge.'

They looked at one another and at the families in the distance, who again moved away south.

'Won't those people join us?' said Khenpo Nima. 'They'd be safer.'

'They don't think so,' the scout replied timidly. 'The Lhasa road is cut. And . . . they don't want to be with anyone from Jyeko.'

'What's that meant to mean?' snapped Karjen.

'There was talk at Chamdo. They say a party of Chinese soldiers is missing – they went to Jyeko and haven't been seen. There was a captain who came into Chamdo riding alone, completely exhausted. There's a story that the Chinese were caught in the gorges, killed by rocks.'

The monks looked at Karjen, who shifted on his pony among a knot of dark-faced friends.

'They're saying Jyeko murdered them,' the boy added. 'There's soldiers searching. No one wants anything to do with Jyeko. We're bad luck.'

Out of the moment of silence that followed, there came a peculiarly shocking sound. It was Jamie giving a short, bitter laugh.

No one knew what to say, what to suggest. Wangdu rested his hands on the pommel of his wooden saddle, shaking his head. Khenpo Nima peered again at the party heading south, now drawing steadily away from them.

'Where *are* they heading?'

'Not to Lhasa. They're going to India.'

'India?'

'They say hundreds of people are gathering at Moro-La – '

'An army, to throw out the Chinese!'

'It's not an army. They're all going to India.'

'Leaving Tibet?'

'I don't believe that for a moment.'

'That's exile!'

'But that's what they're doing.'

Jamie had stopped laughing; he was looking from one face to another. They were floundering.

'Well, to hell with that!' said Karjen. 'Leave Tibet? No, thank you.'

'Look,' someone shouted. 'Look there! Back there!'

They all looked.

Above the pass they had crossed, far behind, there was a curious grey smudge on the snowfields that rose and discoloured the white clouds above. It was faint at first; they might have missed it. But as the moments passed, it became thicker, blacker, dirtier.

Someone murmured, 'Jyeko's burning.'

*

two

A pain gnaws: we pinch another limb for distraction. As the caravan moved on, the thought of what might have become of Puton in Jyeko was more than Jamie could bear. If he allowed his mind to slink back to her, he'd feel his throat tighten, his eyes sting, his brain throb, the start of panic . . . and in desperation he would drag his unruly thoughts elsewhere. Thus he had given full rein to his less generous feelings about Tibet. This was not so hard: he held all Jyeko responsible for Puton's plight.

He rode in silence over the frozen ground, letting his pony find a path among the burrows of the pica. In the Jyeko throng, Jamie spoke to no one. These people did not look so charming now. The wind had stirred up white dust, filling the wrinkles on every face, leaving every eye bloodshot. Jamie felt no charity for any of them, neither monk nor merchant nor the children who had stoned Puton. His mind filled with grim images that he had, maybe, stored away for this moment of need. Things in Jyeko, in Lhasa; things that were not pleasant.

He recalled the beggar-criminals, miserable amputees. It was a routine punishment to manacle a man's legs and turn him loose without his hands, or his feet, or his eyes. Unable to work, he'd creep from shelter to shelter, begging food. Jamie had seen them in Jyeko: who had done that to them – Wangdu? The only 'police' were there in the monastery. One could not take a life in oh-so-Buddhist Tibet, of course, but he'd heard that monastic officials might flog a thief to within an inch of his life then dump him on a blizzard-swept mountainside at nightfall. It could not strictly be said that they had killed him. Just as it could never be said that a good Tibetan had taken the life of a yak or sheep. There just happened to be a profession of bad Tibetans, despised outcasts, to do the butchery for them. So much for tradition!

He'd heard whisper of other things: of pepper forced under eyelids to obtain confessions; of the ritual sacrifice of babies (could that really be true? Just now Jamie was disposed to believe it); of the huge Lhasa monasteries where, it was rumoured, a steady supply of young novices was buggered ragged by the monks. An Indian government doctor in New Delhi had worked in Lhasa and warned him, 'There's hardly a Tibetan doesn't have the clap. Believe it, sir! When their husbands are away they'll fornicate with his brothers – the nearest merchant, the meanest shepherd will do. I've treated ghastly things...'

Jamie had been told things that he'd not credited – until he saw them in Lhasa. People copulating openly on rooftops in the summer sun. Monks from rival monasteries fighting in the streets with wooden clubs. The squalor of the city lanes where everyone upped skirts and shat as they liked. The filth of the houses, where women gave birth in piss-soaked stables then licked their babies clean. The sheer ignorance! A land without carts, without roads, without newspapers, without curiosity. Without maps, even: they scarcely knew the shape of their own country. Half of Tibet thought the earth was flat, and the other half didn't care one way or the other. As for Khenpo Nima's 'medicine' . . .

Such was the catalogue that went through Jamie's sullen mind as he rode onward. He recalled, with an ironic shiver, how he had 'loved' the place, ignoring the horrors of its 'civilisation'. How he'd laughed along with bandits in Jyeko as they reminisced about killing people. How he'd spent so much time learning the language that he'd hardly considered what was being said. How he'd smiled indulgently at the Lhasa aristocracy with their foppish manners and stupendous brocaded robes, their giggling adulteries, their endless parties and staggering wealth wrung from countless serfs on never-seen estates. How he'd listened to justifications of feudal class and caste, of credulity, sorcery and superstition; how he'd 'understood'. Jolting along in his crude wooden saddle, Jamie grimaced at his own naïveté, at his gullibility. He declared to himself that the scales had fallen from his eyes: the place was medieval, and a stiff dose of China might be no bad thing.

He glimpsed, sour-eyed, the villagers riding near to him. Once, he had sat on a hillside outside Jyeko and mused in grateful affection. Now he could see them in one light only: they had condemned Puton. They had no charity, no shred of common decency. He wanted nothing to do with them. He would ride to Lhasa in silence.

But with the sighting of the smoke came a new

desperation. If he relaxed, an unbearable thought of Puton's fate might rush into his mind. His entire body tensed with necessary anger; possibly by holding himself rigid he could block the reverberations of despair. Jamie wanted only one thing: to be out of Tibet as fast as possible. If it was true that the direct Lhasa road was cut, if they were forced to swing in a loop to the south near to the Sikkim border, that was fine by him. If it meant exile, he'd be delighted to assist. They could sweat and rot in refugee camps, feel their self-esteem evaporate and their blood curdle with malaria; that was entirely acceptable. He just wanted them to decide, then get on with it.

The caravan had come to a halt again. The crowd swilled, clumped and hardened about the core of leaders, who had dismounted and stood in a tight circle in the snow. Meanwhile the animals drifted aimlessly over the plain, because Jyeko could not decide where to go. Were they truly being hunted? Humble, backwater Jyeko? The westward road stood apparently empty and inviting, but perhaps a force of Chinese sat astride it somewhere, waiting for them, who knew where? To the east behind them, their homes were burned. To the north, the disasters at Chamdo. To the south ... what?

'So we push them out of the way,' snarled Karjen, his cronies growling their agreement. 'I think we've shown that we can deal with Chink soldiers.'

'This is a village, not an army,' sighed Wangdu.

'We have fifty good men,' Karjen tried again.

'Karjen, your old blood is all afire and your head's full of smoke,' Khenpo Nima reproved him. 'We have women, children and animals to protect. We are slow and noisy. We have no idea how many Chinese there might be. We *must* avoid them.'

'Isn't it obvious?' called another voice. 'We have to go after those people, whether they want our company or not.'

The other little party was still visible, drawing away rapidly to the south.

The weight of opinion swung back and forth. Was the long southern route possible? Probably. Had they enough food? Probably not. Did they know the route? Maybe. Was the pass at Moro-La open at this time of year? They'd know when they got there. It was uncertain, it was frightening. If there was one thing the Khampas knew very well, it was the difficulties of winter travel. Perhaps Karjen was right after all: they should move forward as fast as possible, and break past whatever Chinese force was on the Lhasa road.

'That is crazy,' said Jamie, rather loudly.

Everyone turned to peer at him. It was the first time he'd spoken up since leaving Jyeko. They were well aware of his feelings for them.

'Do you imagine the Communists are a bunch of incompetent peasants? You're up against something else now. They've just won a war beyond your imagination. They're tough, they're the biggest army in the world, and they're after you. If they've cut the Lhasa road, there's going to be hundreds of men, watching for the first sign of your yaks and your families coming through the hills, with horses, machine-guns, radios . . . '

He stopped, suddenly thoughtful, and glanced at the pack animals behind him. Karjen stamped his feet and glared. The monks regarded each other warily, questioning. Wangdu began: 'Mr Jemmy, at least on the Lhasa road we know where they are. We can have scouts forward and feel our way towards them. If we go south, they could be anywhere. We might run straight into them and not know until they start shooting. They're not going to tell us in which valley they're waiting.'

'Well, they might,' murmured Jamie, frowning more thoughtfully still.

His tone was such that everyone fell quiet. Jamie was still staring at the pack animals.

'Jemmy... ?' began Wangdu.

But Jamie cut him short, shouting inexplicably: 'They will! They bloody will!'

The villagers, bewildered, looked to the monks to explain. But Jamie shouted again: 'Nima, Wangdu, come and see!'

He strode towards his animals, the monks following uncertainly and the villagers' eyes on them. Jamie tugged aside the cords that half smothered the radio box. Without taking the crate off, he eased open the cover and peered inside.

'Look!' he said triumphantly, pointing at the radio that nestled in rolls of old blanket. 'The Chinese pre-set it for us.'

Khenpo Nima and Wangdu peered: it was the same radio as before. What did Jamie mean?

'They've left it on their military frequency.' He was

laughing. 'Don't touch! I can read it off . . .'

He grabbed at his own saddlebag, dug in it for a notepad, scribbled down the setting and held it out to Khenpo Nima. His eyes were shining with a hard glint of excitement and irritation: how could the monk not see the point?

'I don't understand,' said Khenpo Nima.

'They tried this frequency every day.' Jamie spelt it out, the contemptuous edge to his voice blunted by delight at his discovery. 'Six o'clock, regular as clockwork. They were waiting for transmissions, orders, don't you see? Their headquarters at Chamdo has transmitters and this is the frequency.'

'So?' asked Nima.

'Nima, we'll know exactly where they are, they'll tell us! We've got the pedal generator. We can check the radio each evening at six o'clock, we can listen to the orders, we can hear where they're sending their patrols and we can avoid them. It's like a spy, it will lead us to safety.'

A quick muttering began that might have been interest or incredulity. Jamie heard someone say, 'We've got our monks: they can use their divining bones.' And another, replying: 'It didn't work in Jyeko, did it? Maybe oracles can't detect Chinese, not being decent Buddhists, you know.'

They looked to Khenpo Nima: he might know the truth – he'd spoken to the radio each day, he'd seen it work. They waited for his verdict.

'But we won't understand what they are saying,' Nima began weakly.

'Who speaks Chinese?' shouted Jamie. No one stirred. 'You traders, some of you have been right down to Chengdu.'

The crowd stirred now, looking one to another.

'Come on, for pity's sake!' bawled Jamie.

Someone shouted, 'Jamyang Sangay!' and at once three or four others chorused, 'Yes, Jamyang Sangay, he knows Chinese!'

'All right,' called Jamie. 'Jamyang Sangay! Where are you? We need you to listen.'

'I'm here,' replied a rasping, arrogant voice. Jamie looked – and winced. Jamyang Sangay stood with his hands on his hips, head cocked sceptically to one side. He was a large, strongly built, corpulent man. He was the landlord who had turned away Puton.

'You're asking for my assistance, Mr Jemmy?' he said, with a distinct sneer.

'No,' said Jamie. 'I'm asking you to help all Jyeko. The Chinese will speak on the radio each evening. You just have to tell us what they say.'

'And why do we want to do that?'

'Because their commanders will be telling the patrols where to go. If Captain Duan really is after us, he'll report to Chamdo every day, so we'll hear exactly where he's going, and we can avoid him. This is an oracle that detects Chinese.'

Someone laughed; Wangdu glowered at them.

'This means,' said Jamyang Sangay, 'that we go the southern route, right? Which would suit you nicely: have us escort you to Moro-La so you can pop over the border?'

'You go along that Lhasa road and you get yourself cut to pieces,' spat Jamie. 'That would suit me just fine too!'

'Jemmy, please!'

Khenpo Nima stood forward between them. He turned towards the leering bulk of Jamyang Sangay. 'I believe Jemmy is correct. Those people,' he nodded to the receding specks of the other little caravan, 'they're heading for Moro-La, they say many others are also. They've seen the Chinese army in Chamdo, they know how bad it is. If there's a gathering at Moro-La, whether it's an army or even just people heading for India, that's the place to be.'

'Reverence,' said Jamyang Sangay, his voice more respectful, 'only you have seen this radio thing work. Tell us, please, are we to trust it?'

Khenpo Nima glanced at Jamie. He'd known him . . . how long? A year? But what marvels in that year. 'We can trust Mr Jemmy absolutely,' he said. 'The radio can guide us if you will assist, Jamyang Sangay.'

The big merchant peered a moment at Jamie, then nodded. 'All right, if that's what everyone wants.'

A ripple of excitement spread through the villagers.

'Look at this, please,' cried Jamie loudly. Jamyang Sangay's pony stood near his own. From its bridle hung half a dozen white silk prayer flags. 'These are yours?' he called to the merchant.

Jamyang Sangay narrowed his eyes, frowning. 'Certainly. They ask for Lord Maitreya's blessing,' he replied.

'Then, excuse me, but the radio needs one.'

Before the merchant had realised it, Jamie had untied a flag from the bridle and was heading for the radio mule.

'Now, just a moment!' huffed Jamyang Sangay.

'Please.' Jamie held up a hand. 'Just watch.'

He pulled open the lid of the case again, extracted three sections of lightweight aerial and fitted them together with quick, practised hands. He tied the white triangular flag to one end, then jammed the aerial down the side of the pack. It stuck straight up, the flag caught at once by the wind.

'Follow this!' cried Jamie. 'Follow the radio flag!' He cursed the villagers, their teetering indecision. They *would* go: he would push them, drag them! He marched to his own pony, swung up into the saddle with the mule's leading rope in his hand and pulled both animals barging out of the throng. He pointed the pony southward and shouted: 'Moro-la! To Moro-la!'

'Moro-la!' bawled Khenpo Nima firmly, striding towards his own animals. The obedient novices went straight after him, and the decision was made. The caravan turned south.

*

The ground began to rise. The wind knocked and buffeted the riders, exhausting them, while the sky ahead took on a lurid purple, thick as swags of velvet. Across these sombre drapes flickered distant lightning.

The wind gusted and picked up the snow in handfuls to throw it in the Khampas' faces. The crystals were small and hard, like sharp sand. They rode with their hats lowered and the horses hung their heads, tossing and blinking with discomfort. The picas stayed fast in their burrows, the griffon vultures and lammergeyers kept to their crags.

In the caravan, all conversation ceased. Jamie tugged the red scarf tighter at his neck and pulled down his hat until the fur pricked his eyes. He could hardly see the way ahead but the pony trudged onward. There was little escape from his thoughts. He sank into his coat like a winkle whose shell would not save it from the pin. Brooding, he felt sick with grief; he thought it unkind that he should be afflicted simultaneously with petrifying cold from without and nausea from within. His senses were cruelly occupied by memory: of the touch and scent of a breast topped by a near-black nipple, of dark slanting eyes, of fluids and scents. He was scarcely aware of present physical sensation except the swill of saliva in the back of his mouth, that told him he was near to retching with misery. He paid no attention to his riding. The reins hung loose in his hand and his body subsided, shivering. He folded in on himself, as though he might have curled into a ball on the saddle and slept.

He was roused by men calling and by the caravan halting for the night. He saw that they had made some progress, that they were not so far from the mountains. He realised how cold he was, chilled to the bone, so he dismounted and threw himself into the business of tents, fires and the radio. He'd dragged Jyeko into the southern route with this promise; he'd have to play it out.

He heaved the radio case inside the black tent with the box that held the pedal dynamo and assembled it; then he went outside and erected the whip aerial. He saw Khenpo Nima watching him, and called: 'Nima! I need someone to crank the generator. Quickly!'

In the spacious tent, an energetic but nervous young man set his back against a saddle pack and his feet on the pedals of the dynamo. On a rug by the radio sat Khenpo Nima, Wangdu, Jamie and his least favourite Khampa, Jamyang Sangay, all cross-legged. Others crowded in. Shortly before six, Jamie waved at the young man to start pedalling.

The flywheel spun, a low whistling coming from the covers. There came a low sigh of satisfaction as the dials began to glow: this alone must have efficacy against the Chinese. As Jamie touched switches and knobs, an electric hiss filled the tent. And then, suddenly, voices.

'Eh? What's that?' Jamyang Sangay sat back in surprise.

'Listen!' commanded Jamie.

The voices were startlingly clear.

'What are they saying, Sangay?' someone whispered.

'I can't make it out,' said the merchant plaintively.

'Listen to them!' snapped Khenpo Nima. 'It's Chinese, isn't it?'

'Yes, yes!'

Flustered, Jamyang Sangay frowned and stared ferociously at the radio. The listeners strained to catch the words.

'That's Chinese all right,' a woman said. 'Where are they?'

'Hush, for pity's sake!' cried Jamie.

'Sangay, listen!' commanded Wangdu.

The stream of messages continued, rapid and staccato. Jamie glanced at Jamyang Sangay questioningly; the merchant was concentrating furiously and leaning forward as though to listen with the very pores of his cheek.

'Something about Batang? Something about transporting ammunition up from Batang. Who's this talking, then? Calls himself Yellow Nine . . .'

'They'll use code names.'

'What?' Sangay grimaced. 'Now I've got Yellow Two.'

'Listen, Sangay!' Khenpo Nima shuffled closer, his nerves fraying.

There was silence for a moment, then another voice began, clearer.

'Now what's he saying?'

'Ssssh!'

'"Blue Nine, where are you? Blue Nine, where are you?" Why do they say everything twice?'

'Blue Nine,' whispered Jamie. 'That's what Duan used in Jyeko.'

'Murderous shit!'

The villagers cocked their ears; if it was Duan, his voice was unrecognisable.

'Where is he, Sangay?'

'I don't know, do I? I'm listen . . . Gyamotang! He says he's in Gyamotang, that's on the Lhasa road. That's exactly where we were going!'

'Ah!' A warm breath of approbation from Khenpo Nima, who patted Jamie's shoulder.

'Listen! What's his orders?'

'He's waiting. The other fellow is asking, any signs? Any riders? . . . He says, "Negative contact." He wants to wait two more days. Then east. He wants to move east.'

'Towards us!'

'We're off his road now.'

'Sssh!'

'The other man says that's good . . . Now it's about ammunition from Batang again. That's it.'

The dynamo man lifted his feet off the pedals, which turned for a few seconds more with a dying hum.

'Well!' said Jamie to the company. 'You see? We'll hear every move he makes.'

'Jemmy, well done,' said Khenpo Nima quietly, and the villagers chorused: 'Well done!'

'Send a message to Lhasa, Jemmy!' cried Karjen. 'Tell them we're coming!'

'Greetings to His Holiness!' called another.

'Tell the Chinese to screw themselves!' shouted a youth.

'Karjen,' began Jamie, 'if I transmit, who will hear?'

'His Holiness.' Karjen smiled, delighted.

'Maybe. Who else?'

'All the spirits!'

'And?'

Karjen subsided, looking uncertain.

'The Chinese?' asked Khenpo Nima.

'Just so,' said Jamie. 'Nobody touches this transmitter – or they'll track us all the way to Moro-La.'

That night Jamie lay in the dark under his swaddling

of quilts and furs, listening to Karjen snore. A dull satisfaction stayed with him. This was how it would be: he would set himself to it, escape and survival, the road to India. He would not abandon anyone, he would get these people to Moro-La: it would occupy his mind and garrison it against misery. After Moro-La they could do what they bloody well liked.

Outside the tent, the wind had not given up. Over the taut fabric it tossed hard grains of snow with a dry sugary rattle. It whispered the threat of the winter road. The temperature was plunging; Hector whined piteously. Without leaving his bed, Jamie reached out and opened the flap a fraction. The mastiff slipped inside at once, shook off the snow and lay by the radio. The huge dog, trained to knock a man from a running horse and a match for most wolves, was reduced to a shivering heap peering round pathetically in the darkness. In his nest of furs, Jamie drew up his legs for warmth. For a terrible moment he thought of fires, and then of fireplaces and houses and houses on fire and then . . . Mercifully, exhaustion claimed him.

He slept fitfully. But the whole chilly camp woke early, creeping out into a clinging grey mist. By Khenpo Nima's baggage a mule lay frozen on the ground, its eyes clouded over.

*

about the **author**

Jonathan Falla

Jonathan Falla has spent much of his life abroad, from his birth in Jamaica, to his career as a paediatric nurse, which has taken him, as part of medical teams, to some of the most vulnerable regions of the world. In Burma he spent a year illegally training paramedics for rebel tribes. He has written plays, short stories and a musical, all influenced by his experiences in countries where conditions are harsh and politics brutal. He is a regular contributor to *Scotland on Sunday* and has recently completed a second novel. He lives in Fife.

'I was born in the Caribbean in 1954, a "white Jamaican" of academic parents. At this moment, the French were losing the battle of Dien Bien Phu and old-style colonialism was dying. It was also the year that the term "Third World" was invented. I came of optimistic liberal stock that envisaged the old world actively helping to construct the new.

I had a public-school-and-Cambridge education, highly qualified in the arts and not very employable.

I spent nearly three years in Java – oddly enough, in Bandung, the very city where the term "Third World" was born – working for a local publisher but spending much of my time learning to play exotic musical instruments and following a puppet troupe into the mountains for all-night performances on rickety bamboo stages in lamplit villages.

At a week's notice Oxfam sent me to a famine in Uganda, roaring around the bush in trucks laden with aid. It was a surreal experience, including a morning handing out three biscuits apiece to felons in the local jail. I came home and turned my diaries into a play which has had many productions. I believe "Topokana Martyrs Day" to be, to date, the only successful comedy about famine relief.

I trained as a nurse in order to work abroad again. Twenty years later, rather to my astonishment, I am still a nurse. It has done me well; I've worked for a rebel tribe in Burma, and for Save the Children in Sudan and Nepal. There was also a year at a film school in Los Angeles. It did me well also as a continuing fund of stories and dramas.

I do have other interests. My wife and baby, and also music. For three years I've been one of a quartet performing professionally around Scotland, playing the lute, recorders and singing baritone in concerts of Renaissance Spanish, French, Italian and Shakespearian music.'

discussion **points**

1. Would you consider *Blue Poppies* to be 'anti-Chinese'? Given their record in Tibet, should it be?

2. Falla has stated that *Blue Poppies* began life as a film script. Is this apparent from aspects of the detail and the structure?

3. Do you have sympathy for the view that such a medieval society needed to be dragged into the twentieth century?

4. What notions of Tibet did you have before reading the book? Did the novel change them?

5. Khenpo Nima betrays his people. Was he justified?

6. An American reviewer has described Falla's prose as cool and unemotional. Do you agree?

press **quotes**

'Jonathan Falla's debut novel, *Blue Poppies*, utterly confounds the stereotype. It is assured, confident, without a trace of self-indulgence. It knows where it's going from the start, and that's nowhere near home ... You'll be lucky to read a finer novel this year.'
– *Scotsman*

'Falla is a fine and unflowery writer who delivers a punchy plot, free of misty-eyed sentiment, yet it is crowned with one of this year's saddest endings.'
– *Sunday Herald*

'... an engaging historical tale intelligently and imaginatively told.'
– *Times Literary Supplement*

'His vivid and authoritative fiction offers us the chance to experience – from the inside – life beyond Western-frontiers, beyond Western preconceptions. In his company, we cease to be newspaper-skimmers or camera-swinging tourists, and go straight to the heart of cultures that are exhilaratingly, sometimes frighteningly different from our own.'
– Michel Faber, author of *Under the Skin*

similar **reads**

Dust on the Paw by Robin Jenkins
(Richard Drew Publishing; ISBN: 0862671485)
A tense, politically disturbing story of inter-racial marriage, set in Afghanistan before the Russian invasion.

Paraja by Gopinath Mohanty
(Faber and Faber; ISBN: 0571151280)
A tragic story of a peasant community in the hill country of Koraput in India, which is turned upside down by a local official's desire for one of the village women.

Wild Swans by Jung Chang
(Flamingo; ISBN: 0006374921)
A searing autobiographical account of life in Communist China by the daughter of party officials.

A Town Like Alice by Neville Shute
(House of Stratus; ISBN: 1842323008)
A mesmerising description of a couple's search for
each other after meeting as prisoners of war in South
East Asia.

Black Narcissus by Rumer Godden
(Pan; ISBN: 0330324705)
A claustrophobic, broodingly sinister fictional
account of a colony of Western nuns living in the
Himalayas.

Miracle on the River Kwai by Ernest Gordon
(Fontana; ISBN: 0006210635)
The autobiographical account of a Scottish soldier
taken prisoner after the fall of Singapore in the
Second World War and forced to help build the
infamous Burma-Siam railroad.

competition

Your chance to win ten contemporary works of fiction signed by their authors.

The *Read Around Books* series was developed by Scottish Book Trust to encourage readers to widen their reading interests and discover writers they had never tried before. Has it been a success? We want to hear from you. Tell us if you have enjoyed this little series or not and if you did, do you have any suggestions for authors who should be included in the series in the future.

Writer to us now with the following information:

Name and address
Email address
Are you a member of a readers' group?
Name of readers' group

Send us the information above and we will enter you into our prize draw to be drawn on 22 August 2003.

Send to:
RAB Draw
Scottish Book Trust
137 Dundee Street
Edinburgh EH11 1BG

scottish **book trust**

What is Scottish Book Trust?

Scottish Book Trust exists to serve readers and writers in Scotland. We work to ensure that everyone has access to good books, and to related resources and opportunities.

We do this in a number of ways:

- By operating the Writers in Scotland Scheme, which funds over 1,400 visits a year by Scottish writers to a variety of institutions and groups
- By supporting Scottish writing through a programme of professional training opportunities for writers
- By publishing a wide variety of resources and leaflets to support readership
- By promoting initiatives such as National Poetry Day and World Book Day
- And through our Book Information Service, providing free advice and support to readers and writers, and the general public.

For more information please visit
www.scottishbooktrust.com

titles **in the series**

Available in the Read Around Books series

Iain Crichton Smith's *Murdo: The Life and Works,*
  by Douglas Gifford

Meaghan Delahunt's *In The Blue House,*
  by Gavin Wallace

Michel Faber's *Under the Skin,* by Mary Firth

Jonathan Falla's *Blue Poppies,* by Rosemary Goring

Janice Galloway's *Clara,* by David Robinson

Andrew Greig's *That Summer,* by Alan Taylor

Anne MacLeod's *The Dark Ship,* by Lindsey Fraser

Maggie O'Farrell's *After You'd Gone,* by Rosemary Goring

Suhayl Saadi's *The Burning Mirror,*
  by Catherine McInerney

Ali Smith's *Hotel World,* by Kathryn Ross

Muriel Spark's *The Comforters,* by Alan Taylor

Alexander Trocchi's *Young Adam,* by Gillian Mackay